FOLK ART
CROSS STITCH
DESIGNS

FOLK ART
CROSS STITCH
DESIGNS
A COLLECTION OF INSPIRATIONAL PROJECTS

DOROTHY WOOD

Photographs by Lucy Mason

HERMES
HOUSE

This edition first published in 1997 by Hermes House

© Anness Publishing Limited 1997

Hermes House is an imprint of
Anness Publishing Limited
Hermes House
88-89 Blackfriars Road
London SE1 8HA

This edition distributed in Canada by
Raincoast Books
8680 Cambie Street
Vancouver
British Columbia
V6P 6MG

ISBN 1 901289 85 0

A CIP catalogue record for this book is available from the
British Library.

Publisher: Joanna Lorenz
Project Editor: Joanne Rippin
Designer: Janet James
Photographer: Lucy Mason
Charts: Ethan Danielson

Printed and bound in Hong Kong

1 3 5 7 9 10 8 6 4 2

CONTENTS

TECHNIQUES: BEGINNING

PREPARING THE FABRIC

Many of the projects in this book use evenweave fabrics which tend to fray easily, therefore it is advisable to finish the edges before starting the embroidery. An allowance has been made for neatening the edges in calculating the materials needed.

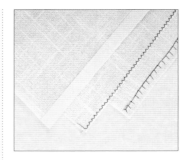

MASKING TAPE

A quick method for projects worked on inter-locking bar frames. The tape can be stapled or pinned to a frame.

ZIGZAG

Machine-stitched zigzag is used when embroidering parts of a garment since the seams will be neatened ready to stitch together.

BLANKET STITCH

This is the best all round method of neatening evenweave fabric. Either turn a small hem or stitch round the raw edge.

LEFT TO RIGHT: masking tape, zigzag and blanket stitch.

COVERING A HOOP

Embroidery hoops (frames) have two rings, one is solid and the other has a screw-fastening. The fabric is sandwiched between the two rings and the screw-fastening adjusted to keep the fabric taut. In order to protect the fabric and stitches from damage, the inner ring is wrapped with narrow cotton tape. Remember that some delicate fabrics can be damaged in an embroidery hoop (frame). In these cases it is advisable to use a large hoop which extends beyond the cross stitch area. Interlocking bar frames are ideal for small projects and a rotating frame is best for large pieces of work.

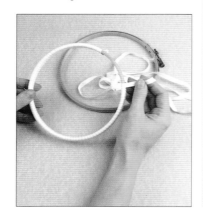

STARTING & FINISHING THREADS

There are several ways to begin a piece of cross stitch. Finish by sliding the needle under several stitches and trimming the end.

1 Fold a length of cotton in half and thread into the needle. Work the first half of the cross stitch, then thread the needle through the loop on the reverse side.

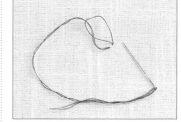

2 Leave a length of 5 cm (2 in) thread at the back of the fabric and weave this in when you have worked a block of stitches.

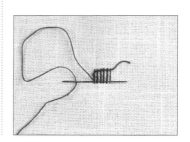

WASTE CANVAS

This technique allows charted cross stitch to be worked on non-evenweave fabric or ready-made items such as towels and cushions. Waste canvas is specially made so that the threads can be easily removed. It is only available in 10 and 14 count but you could use ordinary canvas provided that the threads are not interlocked.

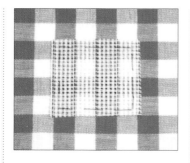

1 Tack (baste) a piece of canvas onto the area to be stitched. Make sure there will be plenty of canvas round the design once it is complete.

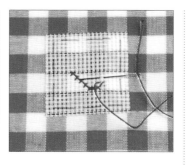

2 Work the cross stitch design over the canvas and through the fabric. Take care to make all the stitches as even as you possibly can.

3 Once complete, fray the canvas and pull the threads out one at a time. It will be easier if you tug the canvas gently to loosen the threads.

TECHNIQUES: FINISHING

MITRED CORNER

Tablecloths and mats can be finished neatly with mitred corners. These reduce bulk and make a secure hem which can be laundered safely.

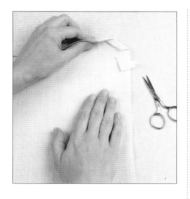 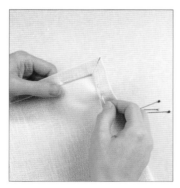

1   Fold the hem, run your fingers along and open out. Cut across the corner from crease to crease and refold the hem.

2   Turn under a further 0.5 cm (¼ in) and pin the hem in place. Slip stitch the mitred corner and machine or hand stitch the hem.

STRETCHING

As a general rule embroidery should always be stretched using thread so that it can be easily removed and cleaned in the future. However, small projects which may be kept for only a limited time can be quickly and successfully mounted using double-sided tape.

1   Cut the card (cardboard) to the required size and stick double-sided tape along all the edges. Trim across the corners and remove the paper backing. Stretch the fabric onto the tape and mitre the corners neatly.

MOUNTING

If a project such as a sampler or picture is likely to be kept for a long time, great care should be taken in mounting the finished work. Acid-free mount board (backing board) or paper should be used under the embroidery and glue or tape which leave an acid residue on the fabric should be avoided.

The following easy method of mounting ensures that the embroidery will be absolutely straight and exactly where you want it.

1   Cut the mount board to size and mark the mid point across the top and bottom of the board. Allow for a wider border at the bottom if required. Mark the mid point of the embroidery at each side of the board and draw in the lines. Lay the embroidery face down on a flat surface and place the mount board on top of it.

2   Line up the guide-lines on the embroidery with the lines on the board. Fold the top edge over and put a pin into the mount board at the centre line. Stretch the fabric slightly and put another pin at the bottom. Repeat the process at the sides. Work your way along each edge from the centre out putting in pins every 2.5 cm (1 in) keeping the grain of the fabric straight.

3   Using a long length of double thread, sew from side to side spacing the stitches about 12 mm (½ in) apart. Join in more thread using an overhand knot. Once complete lift the threads up one at a time to pull them tight and secure. Mitre or fold the corners and repeat along the remaining sides.

ADDITIONS

Most embroidery is embellished by the addition of trimmings, and cross stitch is no exception. Whether it is an Asian design with shisha mirrors and tassels or a traditional English lavender bag edged with Victorian lace, the "additions" always enhance the cross stitch design and add the finishing touch to an attractive piece.

BEADS

Beads are attached using a double thread and in contrast to all other forms of embroidery, begun with a securely tied knot. Sew the beads on individually, as if you were stitching the first half of a cross stitch.

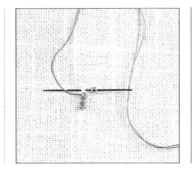

BUTTONS

Buttons with four holes can be stitched on with a large cross stitch to make a very attractive addition to a design.

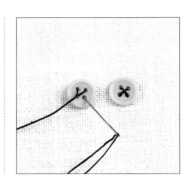

RIBBON

Ribbon looks very effective when used to create a grid for a repeat design of small cross stitch motifs. The ribbon is laid straight along the grain before the cross stitch has been worked. Choose a ribbon which is the same width as one cross stitch. If the ribbon is to be applied diagonally it is easier to work the cross stitch motifs first.

1 Pin the strips of ribbon in position in one direction and pin the rest across the top. Check that the spacing is correct, then tack the ends.

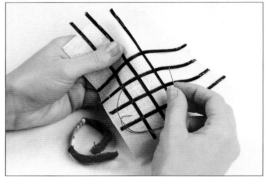

2 Sew a cross stitch at each junction where the ribbons overlap. Remember that if the ribbons are applied diagonally, the cross stitch will be upright.

MAKING A CORD

Embroidery threads are ideal for making into fine cord. The threads can be all one colour or mixed colours to match each particular project.

The amount of thread you need depends on the final thickness of the cord required. As a rough guide, a 1 m (39 in) length of threads ready to twist will make a cord about 40 cm (16 in) long.

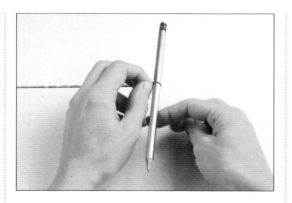

1 Cut several lengths of thread, two and a half times the final cord length. Fix one end to a secure point. Slip a pencil through the threads at the other end and twist the pencil like a propeller.

2 Keep turning until the cord begins to twist together. Hold the middle of the cord and bring the ends together. Smooth any kinks with your fingers and tie the ends with an overhand knot.

SHISHA MIRROR

These irregular pieces of mirror are stitched on to garments and hangings as a protection against evil. If spirits see themselves reflected in the mirror then, it is believed, they will flee.

Traditional shisha mirrors can be bought from ethnic suppliers, but large modern sequins are a suitable alternative. As extra security, stick the mirror or sequins in position using a small piece of double-sided tape or a dab of glue.

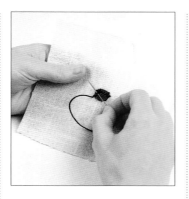

1 Sew two threads across the shisha from top to bottom. Sew across the shisha in the other direction looping the thread round each laid thread to create a framework.

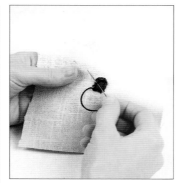

2 Bring the needle up close to the shisha, make a loop through the framework, cross over the loop and pull the thread gently towards you. Take the needle back to the reverse side.

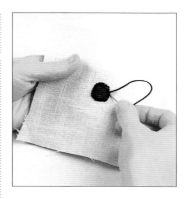

3 Continue round the shisha beginning each stitch between the ends of the previous loop. Finish the thread off on the reverse side.

MAKING TASSELS

One of the prettiest ways to complete a project is to make your own tassels from threads which were used in the embroidery. There are many different ways to make tassels, but most use the same basic technique.

The two following methods are both easy to make. The first tassel is ideal for stitching on to the corners of cushions, mats or bookmarks whereas the second is worked over the end of a cord or rouleau and produces a very professional result. Make the tassels more ornate by adding beads or stitching rows of interlocking blanket stitch round the head until it is completely covered.

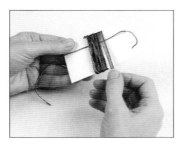

1 Cut a piece of card (cardboard) slightly deeper than the finished length of the tassel. Wind threads round the card as required and slip a length of thread underneath.

2 Cut along the bottom of the threads and tie the bundle together using a sailor's knot. This is like a reef knot, but the thread is twisted round twice before pulling it tight.

3 Wrap another length of thread round the tassel to form a neck and tie off as before. Trim the ends neatly.

1 Wind threads round the card (cardboard) and cut along one side. Tie a knot near the end of the cord or rouleau and place it in the middle of the bundle of threads.

2 Enclose the knot with the threads and tie a separate length of thread around just above the knot.

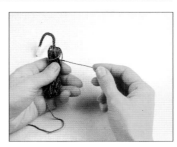

3 Hold the cord and bring all the threads down together. Wrap a length of cord round underneath the knot and tie off securely as before. Trim the tassel ends neatly.

SHAKER BOX

These oval beechwood boxes were used by the Shakers to hold all sorts of things. They can be waxed or painted to match the fabric cover.

YOU WILL NEED

20 x 25 cm (8 x 10 in) maroon 18 count Aida

tacking (basting) thread

needle

embroidery hoop (frame)

Anchor Nordin 150, 275, 316

tapestry needle

beechwood box

paper

pencil

scissors

15 x 20 cm (6 x 8 in) thin wadding (batting)

double-sided tape

60 cm (24 in) of 15 mm (⅝ in) cream ribbon

60 cm (24 in) of 12 mm (½ in) navy ribbon

WORKING THE CROSS STITCH

Tack (baste) along the centre line of the Aida in both directions and work the cross stitch using the thread as it comes, then complete the backstitch.

	Anchor Nordin		Backstitch
⁊⁊	275	—	316
◼	150	☆	Middle point

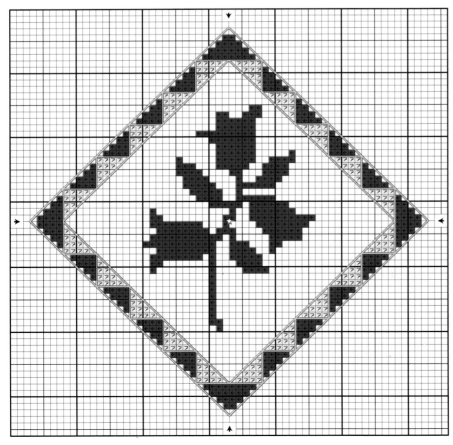

1 To make up: draw round the lid to make a template. Use this to cut out an oval of wadding (batting). Stick it onto the lid. Cut out the cover adding a 1 cm (⅜ in) allowance. Put some double-sided tape round the lid. Centre the design and stretch the fabric down the sides.

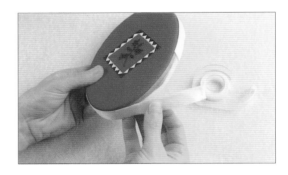

2 Put another layer of tape round the rim and stick on the cream ribbon. Trim and butt the ends together.

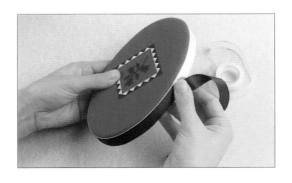

3 Repeat this process with the blue ribbon, leaving a touch of cream showing. This time turn under the raw end and stick it down.

NINE STAR PICTURE

A simple design inspired by early American patchwork heart and star pictures.

YOU WILL NEED

46 cm (18 in) square of antique white 28 count Cashel linen, Zweigart E3281

vanishing marker pen

tracing paper

pencil

paper scissors

tacking (basting) thread

needle

stranded cotton Anchor 39, 150, 169, 246, 305

tapestry needle

30 cm (12 in) square of mount board (backing board)

strong thread

frame

WORKING THE CROSS STITCH

Mark a 25 cm (10 in) square in the middle of the linen and stitch the border design, sewing 20 hearts across and 24 down. Fold the fabric in half both ways to find the centre and mark with the vanishing marker pen. Work the heart cross stitch pattern within the lines beginning with a heart on the centre mark.

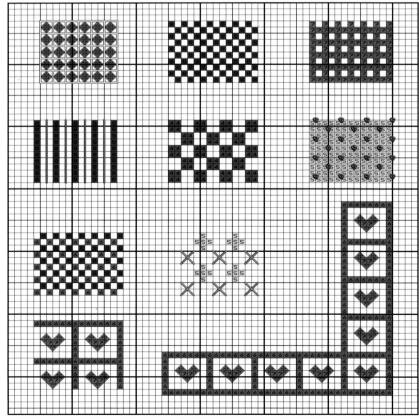

1. To make up: trace and cut out the star template. Place in the centre of the border and draw round it carefully with the pen.

2. Following the grain of the fabric make a second mark on the left 8 cm (3 in) from the centre. Draw round the star template and fill with another cross stitch pattern. Continue in this way, spacing the centres 8 cm (3 in) apart, until all nine stars are complete. Finish the design by stitching a grid of blue running stitch mid way between the stars to make nine equal 8 cm (3 in) boxes.

3. Stretch the linen over the mount board (backing board) and put in a simple frame.

	Anchor	Backstitch
4 4	246	— 39
5 5	305	— 305
6 6	169	— 246
7 7	39	French knots
8 8	150	♥ 150

UTENSIL BOX

This simple box could be used to store candles, paintbrushes or pens and pencils instead of these kitchen utensils.

WORKING THE CROSS STITCH

Tack (baste) guidelines across the centre of the linen in both directions and work the cross stitch using two strands of cotton over two threads. Press the embroidery on the reverse side when it is complete.

1 To make up: paint the box with two coats of dark blue paint. Allow the paint to dry between coats.

2 Trim the card (cardboard) to fit the front of the box. Stretch the linen over it, mitring the corners neatly, and stick the panel onto the front of the box.

YOU WILL NEED

15 x 20 cm (6 x 8 in) 28 count natural evenweave linen

tacking (basting) thread

needle

embroidery hoop (frame)

stranded cotton Anchor 150, 1034, 1036

tapestry needle

scissors

plain utensil box

dark blue emulsion paint

paintbrush

8 x 15 cm (3 x 6 in) thin card (cardboard)

craft knife

all-purpose glue

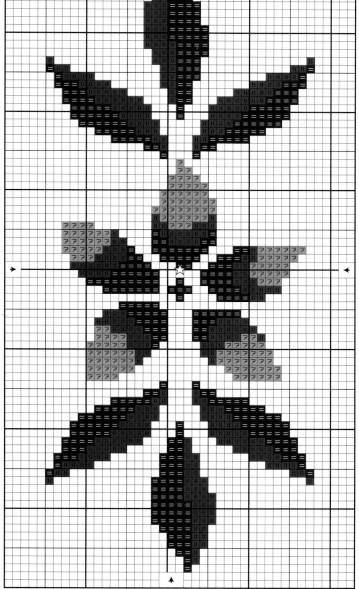

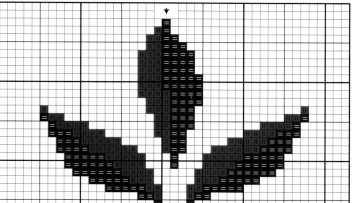

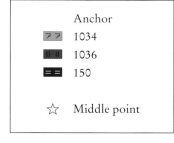

Anchor

⤸⤸ 1034

▮▮ 1036

══ 150

☆ Middle point

HEART VINE WREATH

Make the wreath with fresh Virginia creeper or clematis stems and let it dry out under a weight to hold the heart shape.

YOU WILL NEED

20 x 30 cm (8 x 12 in) antique white 28 count Cashel linen, Zweigart E3281

flexihoop (small embroidery frame)

red Anchor Nordin 47

embroidery needle

15 x 23 cm (6 x 9 in) lightweight iron-on interfacing

scissors

pencil

pins

scraps of different red gingham fabrics

sewing thread

polyester stuffing

Virginia creeper or clematis stems

string

WORKING THE CROSS STITCH

Embroider the six hearts onto the linen using one strand of Nordin over two threads of linen, leaving about 2.5 cm (1 in) round each design.

1 To make up: iron on 8 cm (3 in) squares of interfacing to the reverse side and cut out. Draw a heart on each piece, pin to a square of gingham and stitch. Trim the seams, turn through and stuff then slip stitch the gap.

2 Cut eight 60 cm (24 in) lengths of vine. Split the bundle in two and make into a heart shape securing the ends with vine. Wind some more vine round and round the rest of the wreath to hold it together.

3 Sew a 13 cm (5 in) length of embroidery thread through the back of each heart and use it to tie the hearts round the wreath. Add a loop for hanging or fit over a nail.

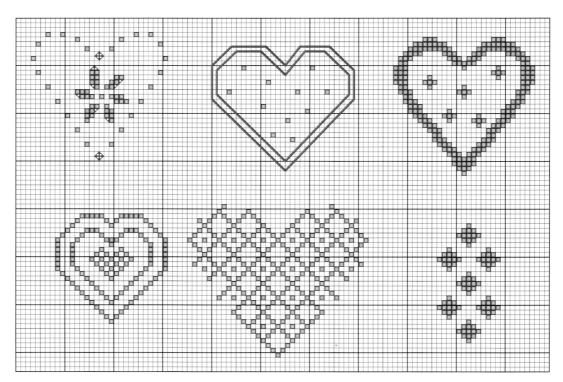

	Anchor Nordin
⊞⊞	47
	Backstitch
——	47

TRAY CLOTH

This cloth has been specially made for the tray but the design could be adapted slightly to a tray of any size.

YOU WILL NEED

ruler

paper

pencil

scissors

four different "fat quarters" of gingham

medium weight iron-on interfacing

sewing machine

sewing thread

fusible bonding web

stranded cotton Anchor Nordin 144

embroidery needle

cotton lining

nine buttons

WORKING THE CROSS STITCH

Measure your tray and using a scaled up template draw out a paper pattern to fit inside. Adding 1.5 cm (⅝ in) seam allowances all round, cut out a triangle and a strip from each of the four kinds of gingham. Iron interfacing to the reverse side of each piece. With right sides facing, sew each pair of triangles together along the short sides and sew two strips together for each end. Stitch the large triangles together to make a square and sew the strips on opposite sides.

1 To make up: cut four hearts from the bonding web and iron onto the reverse side of different ginghams. Cut out leaving a 5 mm (¼ in) seam allowance. Remove the paper, snip the seams, fold over and press.

2 Position the hearts on the tray cloth and iron again. Sew large cross stitches round each heart and along the seams of the triangles and side panels.

3 With right sides together, sew the lining to the mat leaving a gap. Trim the seams and turn through. Slip stitch the gap and press. Sew a button in the centre and space the other buttons down each of the sides to complete.

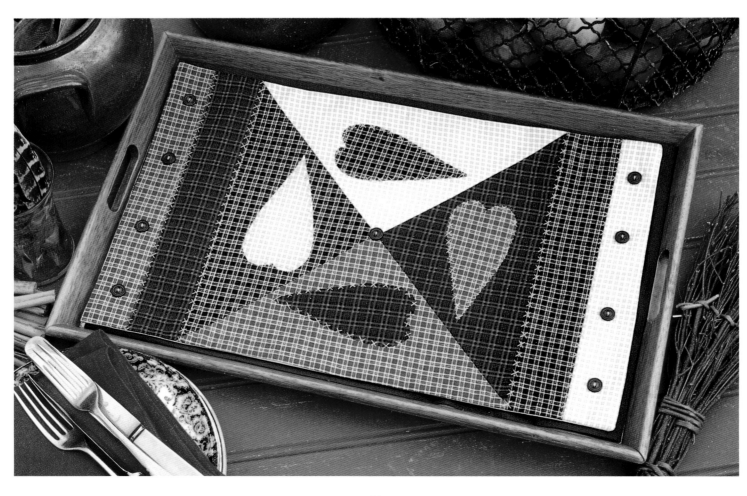

16

CURTAIN PELMET

These delightful geese would be ideal for a child's bedroom. Simply wrap the fabric round a curtain pole or finish with heading tape.

WORKING THE CROSS STITCH

Measure the width of the window and cut a piece of gingham twice as wide and about 50 cm (20 in) deep. Tack (baste) the squares of waste canvas about 15 cm (6 in) apart along the bottom of the fabric, allowing for the hem and side turnings. Try to position the centre lines of the canvas on the same check each time. Work the cross stitch using three strands of cotton.

1 To make up: once the embroidery is complete, carefully remove the canvas threads one at a time and press the fabric on the reverse side.

2 Finish the raw edges at the side of the pelmet and turn under 5 cm (2 in). Turn up the hem of the pelmet and stitch. Add curtain tape along the top edge or simply wrap the fabric round a curtain pole and adjust the gathers.

YOU WILL NEED

tape measure

red, green and cream gingham

scissors

10 count waste canvas, 10 cm (4 in) square for each motif

tacking (basting) thread

needle

stranded cotton Anchor 386, 879, 1006

embroidery needle

sewing thread

curtain tape (optional)

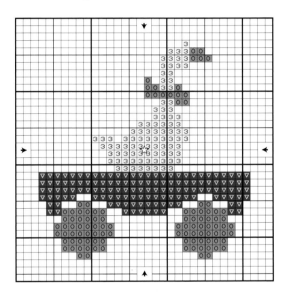

Anchor	
3 3	386
o o	1006
▽ ▽	879
☆	Middle point

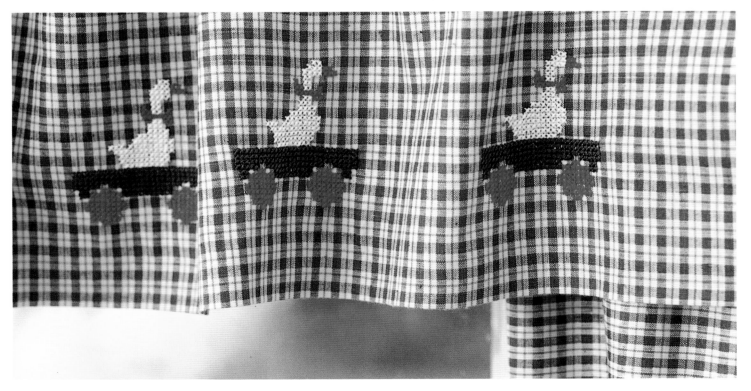

GAME BOARD

This game board is quite easy to make with only basic woodworking skills. It is antiqued using crackle varnish and oil paint.

YOU WILL NEED

30 x 36 cm (12 x 14 in) gold 32 count evenweave linen

scissors

tacking (basting) thread

needle

embroidery hoop (frame)

stranded cotton Anchor white, 44, 170, 211, 403

tapestry needle

28 x 51 cm (11 x 20 in) of 5 mm (¼ in) medium density fibreboard (MDF)

off-white acrylic or emulsion paint

paintbrush

ruler

pencil

blackboard paint

1.6 m (1¾ yd) of 2.5 cm (1 in) wood edging

56 cm (22 in) of 2 cm (¾ in) wood edging

fretsaw

wood glue

masking tape

Craquelure, Steps 1 & 2 varnish

raw umber oil paint

soft cloth

antique brown wax

23 x 28 cm (9 x 11 in) mount board (backing board)

safety ruler

craft knife

double-sided tape

WORKING THE CROSS STITCH

Cut the linen in half lengthways. Tack (baste) guidelines down the centre in both directions and work the cross stitch using two strands of cotton over two threads. Stitch the second piece to match and press on the reverse side.

1 To make up: paint a 28 cm (11 in) square in off-white in the middle of the MDF and allow to dry. Beginning in the middle of one side, mark every 33 mm (1¼ in). Repeat on the other edges and draw out the squares. (There should be an 8 mm (½ in) border all round). Paint the left hand square black, then paint every second square black in alternate rows. When these are dry, paint the remaining black squares.

2 Cut two 51 cm (20 in) pieces and two 28 cm (11 in) pieces from the 2.5 cm (1 in) wood edging. Glue these to the side of the board and hold in place with masking tape. Cut the narrower strip to fit inside and stick down across the board. Paint the completed board with an even coat of the first varnish and allow to dry according to the manufacturer's instructions. Brush on the second varnish which takes a little longer to dry. Cracks will appear but may not be obvious as the varnish is transparent.

3 Next day rub some raw umber oil paint into the cracks with a soft cloth and leave to dry. Rub the entire board with antique brown wax. Measure the end sections and cut the mount board (backing board) slightly smaller. Stretch the embroidery over the mount board and stick securely inside the end sections using double-sided tape to complete.

	Anchor		French knots
11	170	♥	403
--	211		
++	403	☆	Middle point
1 1	1		
22	44		

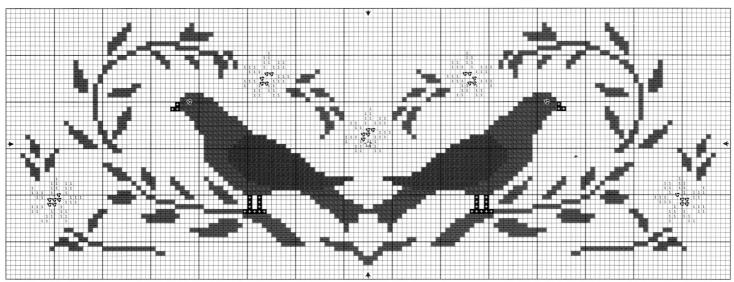

NAPKIN

*The edge of this napkin has been finished with a pretty
two-colour border to match the heart design.*

YOU WILL NEED

*40 cm (16 in) square of
grey/blue 28 count Jobelan*

sewing machine

sewing thread

scissors

*Anchor Nordin 127, 150, 326,
341*

embroidery needle

tacking (basting) thread

needle

embroidery hoop (frame)

WORKING THE CROSS STITCH

Turn under 5 mm (¼ in) round all sides and machine stitch. Mitre
the corners and turn over a further 5 mm (¼ in). Hold the hem
in place with running stitch in dark blue going over and under
four threads at a time. Complete the border with rust. Tack
(baste) a guideline round one corner of the napkin, 3 cm (1¼ in)
in from the edge. Work the cross stitch over two threads and press.

Anchor		
■■ 127	■■ 341	
■■ 150		
■■ 326	☆ Middle point	

HERB DECORATION

This delightful little gingerbread man will cheer up any kitchen and could be filled with a sachet of herbs or potpourri.

WORKING THE CROSS STITCH

Tack (baste) guidelines across the centre of one square of the linen in both directions and work the cross stitch using two strands of cotton over two threads. When complete press on the reverse side.

1 To make up: cut the ribbon in half and pin to the top edge of one square 4 cm (1½ in) apart. Pin the two pieces of linen together with right sides facing, tucking the ribbon inside. Stitch round the sides leaving a 5 cm (2 in) gap at the bottom. Trim the seams and across the corners then turn through.

2 Cut two squares of wadding (batting) the size of the cushion and tuck inside together with a sachet of herbs. Slip stitch the gap closed. Tie a bow for hanging.

YOU WILL NEED

two 16 cm (6¼ in) squares of evergreen 28 count Belfast linen, Zweigart E3609

tacking (basting) thread

needle

interlocking bar frame

stranded cotton DMC 221, 310, 676, 729, 825, 3823

tapestry needle

1 m (1 yd) of 2 cm (¾ in) gingham ribbon

scissors

pins

sewing machine

sewing thread

polyester wadding (batting)

dried herbs or pot pourri

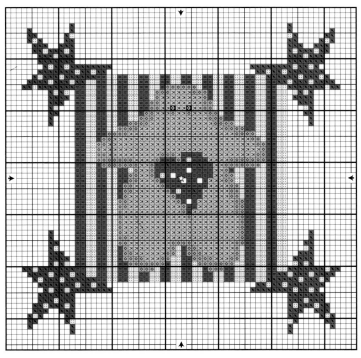

DMC				
221	676	825	☆	Middle point
3823	729	310		

PATCHWORK CUSHION

The motifs on this homespun patchwork cushion are based on nineteenth-century North American samplers.

YOU WILL NEED

nine 13 cm (5 in) squares of different gingham fabrics with approximately 10 squares to 2.5 cm (1 in)

embroidery hoop (frame)

stranded cotton DMC 304, 444, 801, 924, 3821, 3830

embroidery needle

pins

sewing machine

sewing thread

four small pearl buttons

scissors

needle

40 x 60 cm (15 x 24 in) contrast backing fabric

30 cm (12 in) cushion pad

WORKING THE CROSS STITCH

Work the cross stitch using three strands of cotton over each small square. Stitch one orange basket and two of each of the other designs. Once complete, press on the reverse side and lay out the squares on a flat surface to check their positions.

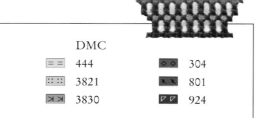

DMC		
== == 444		◇ ◇ 304
⬚⬚⬚ 3821		✖ ✖ 801
⊁ ⊁ 3830		▽ ▽ 924

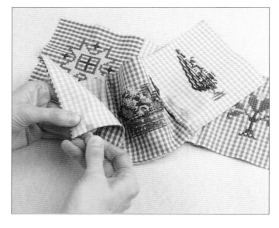

1 To make up: stitch three lots of three squares together with 12 mm (½ in) seam allowances and press the seams open. Pin the rows together matching the seams, stitch and press again. Sew a button at each corner of the centre square.

2 Cut the contrast backing fabric in half to make two 30 x 40 cm (12 x 15 in) rectangles and sew a narrow hem lengthways along one side of each. With right sides together, pin one piece to the left side of the patchwork square and the second piece to the right side. Overlap the hems and sew round all four sides. Trim across the corners and turn through. Tuck the cushion pad inside to complete.

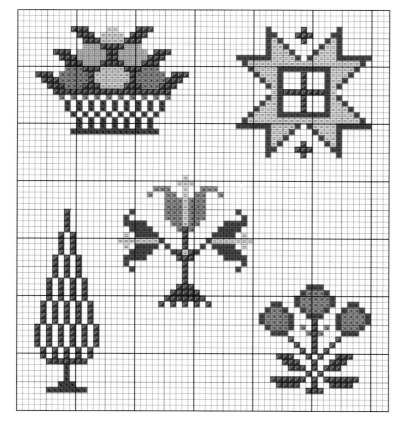

KITCHEN APRON

Everyone will be happy to wear this big, bright apron
with its three cheery gingerbread men.

YOU WILL NEED

large cook's apron

15 x 30 cm (6 x 12 in) 10 count
waste canvas

tacking (basting) thread

needle

coton perlé no.5 DMC 543

embroidery needle

WORKING THE CROSS STITCH

Tack (baste) the waste canvas onto the bib of the apron, positioning it about 8 cm (3 in) down from the top edge. Work the cross stitch as shown through the waste canvas. Once complete remove the tacking thread.

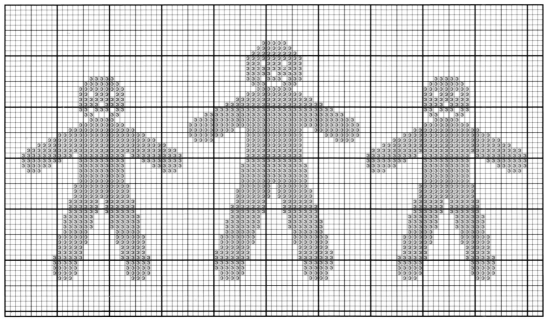

1. To make up: once complete, remove the canvas threads one at a time. You may find it easier to take out the shorter threads first. Press the embroidery on the reverse side.

DMC coton perlé no.5

33	543

24

HAND TOWEL

*Make this pretty border to sew on to a plain waffle towel
and add your own initials.*

YOU WILL NEED

white waffle hand towel

*20 x 90 cm (8 x 36 in)
homespun cotton gingham
with approximately 10 squares
to 2.5 cm (1 in)*

scissors

tacking (basting) thread

needle

*stranded cotton DMC 321,
815, 3808*

embroidery needle

pins

sewing machine (optional)

sewing thread

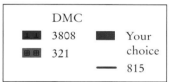

DMC		
3808		Your
321		choice
—	815	

WORKING THE CROSS STITCH

Wash both the towel and the gingham to check for shrinkage. Cut the gingham so that it measures 5 cm (2 in) wider than the towel. Tack (baste) guidelines across the centre of the gingham in both directions and work the cross stitch using three strands of cotton over each square. Stitch your choice of initials first, then work the hearts on either side.

1 To make up: press the embroidery on the reverse side. Trim the long edges so that there is 4 cm (1½ in) on either side of the cross stitch. Press under 12 mm (½ in) on all sides and pin to the end of the towel. Fold the short ends to the back and tack. Hand or machine stitch the gingham close to the edge using matching thread.

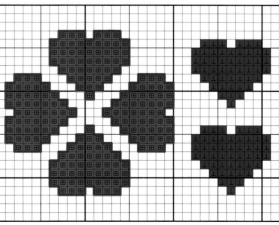

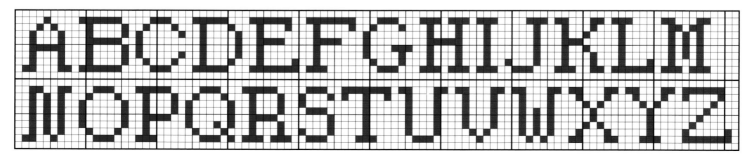

25

WOODEN SPOON MOBILE

Paint an old wooden spoon and make a charming kitchen decoration with some oddments of gingham and embroidery cotton.

YOU WILL NEED

three 8 cm (3 in) squares of different gingham fabric

three 5 cm (2 in) squares of 14 count waste canvas

tacking (basting) thread

needle

six 10 cm (4 in) squares of contrast gingham

8 x 25 cm (3 x 10 in) fusible bonding web

scissors

Anchor Nordin 13, 134, 281

embroidery needle

sewing machine

sewing thread

polyester stuffing

wooden spoon

pencil

hand drill

yellow paint, Colourman 122

paintbrush

adhesive tape

large eye needle

WORKING THE CROSS STITCH

Tack (baste) the waste canvas onto the small gingham squares and work one motif in the centre of each. Remove the waste canvas one thread at a time once the embroidery is finished and press lightly on the reverse side.

1 To make up: iron fusible bonding web on to the reverse side of the squares and trim them to 5.5 cm (2¼ in). Remove the backing paper and iron the embroidered squares onto three squares of the contrast gingham. Work a row of tiny red running stitches round each small square to secure. Sew the backs onto the cushions with right sides facing, leaving open along one side. Trim the corners and turn through. Fill with stuffing and slip stitch to close.

2 Lay the cushions under the spoon and mark the position of the holes. Drill small holes through the spoon and paint with two coats of yellow paint.

3 Make a 60 cm (24 in) cord with Anchor Nordin 281. Cut it in three equal pieces and tape the ends to prevent them unravelling. Thread a cord through each hole and sew the ends into one corner of each cushion.

	Anchor
⁊⁊	134
☐☐	13
→ →	281

PARTY HORSE

Children love to role-play with this traditional folk art doll who is dressed in her Sunday best and ready for a tea-party.

YOU WILL NEED

20 x 30 cm (8 x 12 in) white cotton fabric

tracing paper

pencil

5 cm (2 in) square of 14 count waste canvas

tacking (basting) thread

needle

stranded cotton DMC 799, 3347

embroidery needle

30 cm (12 in) broderie anglaise

pins

scissors

sewing machine

sewing thread

30 cm (12 in) of 5 mm (1/4 in) white ribbon

40 cm (1/2 yd) of 90 cm (36 in) wide natural linen or fine wool

polyester stuffing

two 5 mm (1/4 in) black beads

0.25 m (1/4 yd) of 115 cm (45 in) wide blue cotton print

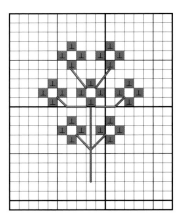

DMC
⊥ 799
Backstitch
— 3347

WORKING THE CROSS STITCH

Trace the apron template onto the white cotton. Tack (baste) the waste canvas in the middle of the lower half and work the cross stitch using three strands of cotton. Remove the waste canvas thread by thread and complete the backstitch as shown. Press the embroidery on the reverse side. Pin the broderie anglaise round the embroidered section of the apron. Fold the apron in half with right sides together and stitch, leaving a gap on one side. Turn through and press. Pin the ribbon across the top of the apron and stitch all round close to the edge.

1 To make up: enlarge the templates and cut out the pattern pieces for the horse. Using 5 mm (1/4 in) seam allowance, stitch the heads, ears, arms and legs together in pairs leaving the short straight edges unstitched. Stuff all the pieces except for the ears. Turn the raw edges inside, pinch the bottom of each ear and hand sew on either side of the head seam.

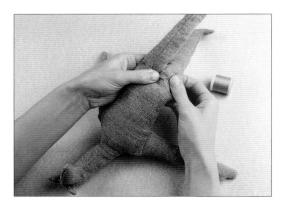

2 For the eyes, stitch on one bead and take the thread through to the other side. Pull it taut to sink the eye slightly and sew on the second bead. Stitch the torso leaving open between the dots and at the top and bottom. Tuck the head inside and slip stitch securely. Attach the arms in the same way, then stuff the body firmly.

3 Pin the legs in place and backstitch through all layers along the bottom of the torso. Cut out the dress bodice and a 20 x 61 cm (8 x 24 in) rectangle for the skirt. Stitch the outer sleeve seam and the underarm seam. Sew a small piece of lace to the neck edge and hem the sleeve ends. Stitch the short ends of the skirt together to form a tube and gather round one end. Pin to the bodice and stitch. Fold under a narrow hem and stitch to complete.

GUEST TOWEL

Screw two brass hooks to the back of a door or hang this unusual guest towel from a row of wooden pegs.

YOU WILL NEED

white waffle hand towel

30 cm (12 in) homespun check fabric with approximately 10 squares to 2.5 cm (1 in)

scissors

tacking (basting) thread

needle

embroidery hoop (frame)

coton perlé no.5 DMC 311, 400, 469, 726, 814

embroidery needle

pins

sewing machine

sewing thread

40 cm (16 in) woven tape

two pearl buttons

WORKING THE CROSS STITCH

Wash the towel and gingham before beginning to check for colour fastness and shrinkage. Cut the gingham 2.5 cm (1 in) wider than the towel. Fold the fabric in half crossways and mark this with a line of tacking (basting). Beginning with the red flower, embroider the motifs 5 cm (2 in) up from the bottom of the fabric. Reverse the motifs for the other side.

1 To make up: with right sides together, stitch the bottom edge of the embroidered panel to the top of the hand towel. Fold and press under a 12 mm (½ in) seam allowance along the top edge. Fold the gingham in half with right sides together, stitch the side seams, then trim and turn through.

2 Slip stitch the folded edge to the back of the towel. Cut the tape in half. Fold into loops and pin the raw edges to each corner of the embroidered panel. Stitch across the bottom of the loop, fold it over on itself and stitch securely. Sew a button to the front of each corner as a trimming.

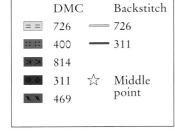

	DMC	Backstitch	
==	726	——	726
∷∷	400	——	311
⟩⟩	814		
◆◆	311	☆	Middle point
⟩⟩	469		

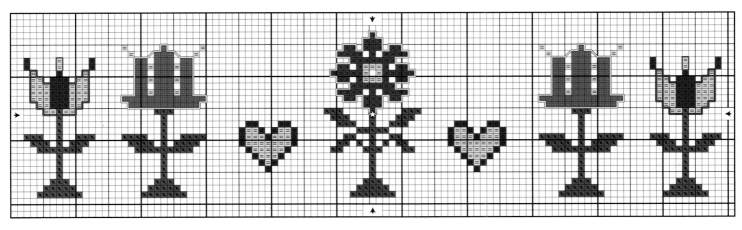

30

FOLK ART COW

*Children will love this traditional folk art style
cow and the bright colourful border.*

WORKING THE CROSS STITCH

Tack (baste) guidelines across the middle of the Aida in both directions. Begin in the middle and work the cow picture. Leave two rows of Aida clear all round for the green ribbon. Next, work the patchwork border.

1 To make up: pin the ribbon round the edge of the cross stitch and in the space left round the cow. Stitch the ribbon to the Aida with tiny hem stitches.

2 Cut the mount board (backing board) slightly larger than the outside ribbon edge. Stretch the embroidery over the board and put into a frame of your choice.

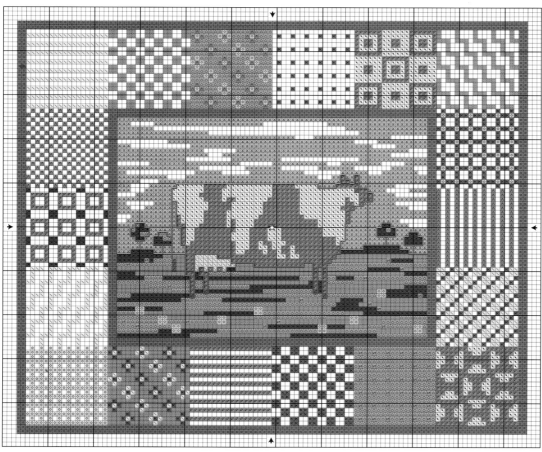

DMC	
═ ═	ribbon
∷ ∷	954
▶ ▶	702
◇ ◇	444
⋈ ⋈	Ecru
▽ ▽	10
╱ ╱	898
╲ ╲	605
⋈ ⋈	603
∧ ∧	553
✕ ✕	799
✕ ✕	827
⌂ ⌂	254 Anchor

Backstitch
— 898

☆ Middle point

HERBS ON A ROPE

Fill these five lovely bags with cinnamon sticks, chilli peppers or dried herbs and hang on the kitchen wall.

YOU WILL NEED

10 x 15 cm (4 x 6 in) white 16 count Aida

scissors

stranded cotton DMC 311, 815

tapestry needle

12 x 20 cm (4¾ x 8 in) dark blue denim

pins

embroidery needle

pinking shears

five 15 x 20 cm (6 x 8 in) rectangles in different red and blue checks

all-purpose glue

sewing machine

sewing thread

cinnamon, chilli peppers and other dried herbs

1 m (1 yd) heavyweight cotton cord

2.5 cm (1 in) brass curtain ring

coarse string

WORKING THE CROSS STITCH

Cut five 4.5 cm (1¾ in) squares out of the Aida. Work a cross stitch heart in the middle of each piece using three strands of cotton and then complete the red cross stitch.

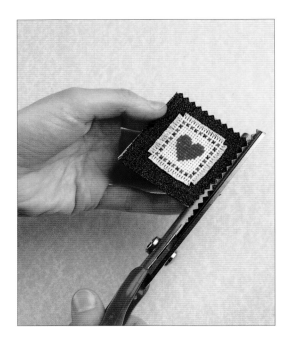

1 To make up: cut five 7 cm (2¾ in) denim squares and pin the embroidered pieces to them. Work the blue cross stitch through both layers. Fray the edge of the Aida squares and trim the edges of the denim with pinking shears. Glue each heart motif to the centre of a check rectangle, 4 cm (1½ in) from the lower edge. Fold in half so that the heart is on the inside and stitch the short edges together. Position the seam at the centre back and press flat. Stitch along the bottom edge, trim the corners and turn through. Trim the tops of the bags with pinking shears and work a row of running stitches 4 cm (1½ in) from the top.

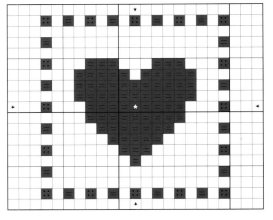

DMC		
■ 815	☆	Middle point
■ 311		

2 Fill with different herbs, pull up the running stitches and fasten securely. Thread the brass ring onto the cord, fold it in half and bind the top with string to secure. Tie the bags onto the double string at intervals using short lengths of string.

EMBROIDERED LAUNDRY BAG

Embroider your own choice of initials in a similar style and make one of these big, useful laundry bags for each member of the family.

YOU WILL NEED

50 cm (20 in) of 6 cm (2½ in) Aida band with red border, Zweigart E7315

stranded cotton DMC 815

tapestry needle

80 x 100 cm (31 x 39 in) white linen or a textured woven cotton

scissors

pins

sewing machine

sewing thread

quilting pencil

needle

2 m (2¼ yd) medium white piping cord

safety pin

comb

WORKING THE CROSS STITCH

Fold the Aida band in half crossways to find the centre and work the cross stitch using three strands of cotton.

1 To make up: cut the white fabric into two 50 x 80 cm (20 x 31 in) rectangles. Pin, then stitch the band to one piece, 20 cm (8 in) from the lower edge.

2 With the embroidered band on the inside, pin the two pieces together. Starting and finishing 20 cm (8 in) from the top, stitch round the sides and along the bottom. Press the seams open and flatten the corners to make a right angled point at each end of the bottom seam. Measure 5 cm (2½ in) in from each point and mark a diagonal line across each corner. Pin and stitch across the corners to form a flat base.

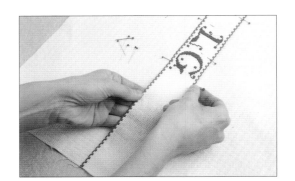

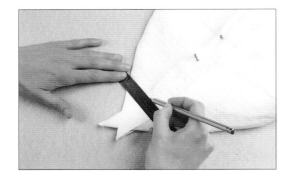

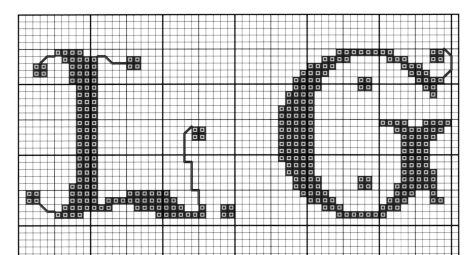

3 Fold over and stitch the seam allowance round both top flaps. Fold in half to the inside and stitch along the edge of the hem. Make a second row of stitching 4 cm (1½ in) up from this to form a drawstring channel. Cut the cord in two and thread through opposite ends of the channel using a safety pin. Knot the two ends of each cord together 8 cm (3 in) from the end. Unravel the ends to form a tassel, comb the ends out and trim neatly.

DMC	Backstitch
▢▢ 815	— 815

SWISS ALPHABET SAMPLER

Samplers worked in a single colour were particularly popular in Europe in the nineteenth century.

YOU WILL NEED

30 x 36 cm (12 x 14 in) white 14 count Aida

tacking (basting) thread

interlocking bar frame

needle

stranded cotton DMC 3 skeins of 304

tapestry needle

23 x 28 cm (9 x 11 in) mount board (backing board)

strong thread

picture frame

DMC	
▬▬	304
☆	Middle point

WORKING THE CROSS STITCH

Tack (baste) guidelines across the middle of the Aida in both directions and work the cross stitch using three strands of cotton. Work the middle row of letters, then those above and below. Finally stitch the border and corner motifs.

1 To make up: once complete, press on the reverse side and trim any ends of thread so that they do not show through on the right side. Stretch the embroidery over the mount board (backing board) and put into a frame of your choice.

SWISS PILLOWCASE

European countries each have their own particular style of cross stitch.
Plain red on white or cream is typical of Switzerland.

YOU WILL NEED

white Oxford pillowcase
25 cm (10 in) 14 count waste
canvas
scissors
tacking (basting) thread
needle
stranded cotton Anchor 47
embroidery needle

❖❖❖❖❖

NEEDLEWORK TIP

The corner design on
this pillowcase will
depend very much on
the length of the border.
Adapt the chart to suit,
if necessary.

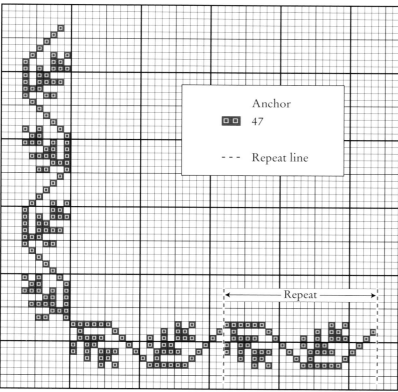

	Anchor
	47
- - -	Repeat line

← Repeat →

1 Cut 2.5 cm (1 in) strips of
waste canvas and tack (baste)
in position round the border of the
pillow-case, 12 mm (½ in) from the
stitching. Beginning in the centre of
one long side, work the cross stitch
using two strands of cotton.

2 Stop when you are near the
corner and plan the design to
fit the corner based on the cross
stitch chart. Complete the other half
of the side to match and then finish
the rest of the stitching. Press the
pillowcase on the reverse side.

POTPOURRI SACHET

The beautiful white Austrian lace adds the finishing touch to this charming little cross stitch design.

YOU WILL NEED

two 13 x 15 cm (5 x 6 in) pieces of white 14 count Aida

stranded cotton DMC 517, 666

tapestry needle

1 m (1 yd) of 4 cm (1½ in) Austrian lace

tacking (basting) thread

needle

pins

15 cm (6 in) narrow red ribbon

sewing machine

sewing thread

scissors

pot pourri sachet

two 10 x 13 cm (4 x 5 in) pieces of wadding (batting)

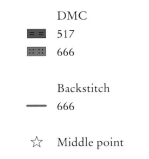

DMC	
▦	517
▦	666

Backstitch	
—	666

| ☆ | Middle point |

WORKING THE CROSS STITCH

Find the centre of the Aida and work the cross stitch using two strands of cotton and the backstitch using one strand. Press on the reverse side.

1 To make up: gather the lace and pin round the edge of the embroidered panel. Adjust the gathers and tack. Fold the ribbon in half and pin to a top corner with the loop facing inward.

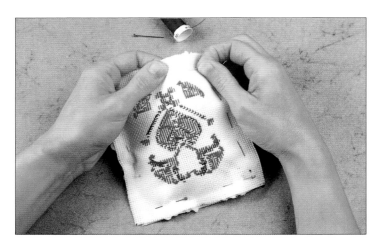

2 With the embroidery and lace to the inside, stitch round three sides. Trim the seams and corners and turn through. Put the pot pourri sachet between the layers of wadding (batting) and insert into the cushion. Slip stitch the opening to finish.

SHELF BORDER

Red and blue cross stitch is very popular in Eastern Europe where the carnation is a traditional motif.

YOU WILL NEED

7 cm (2³⁄4 in) bleached linen blue-edged band, Inglestone collection 950/70

stranded cotton Anchor 161, 1006

tapestry needle

sewing thread

needle

Anchor	
⠿	1006
═ ═	161

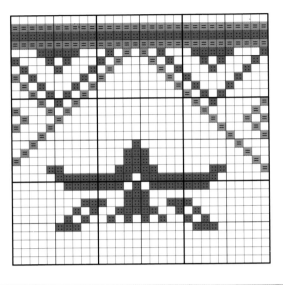

WORKING THE CROSS STITCH

The amount of band and stranded cotton required will depend on the length of your shelf.

1 To make up: fold the band in half crossways and begin stitching the design in the centre six threads down from the border. Continue, then repeat out to both ends of the linen band.

2 Press on the reverse side and stitch a narrow hem at each end to finish the raw edges.

BEDSIDE TABLECLOTH

This versatile design could be stitched onto napkins or on each corner of a much larger tablecloth.

YOU WILL NEED

46 cm (18 in) square of antique white 28 count Cashel linen, Zweigart E3281

tacking (basting) thread

needle

stranded cotton DMC three skeins of 311, one of 3350

tapestry needle

embroidery hoop (frame)

scissors

sewing thread

8 cm (3 in) square of card (cardboard)

WORKING THE CROSS STITCH

Tack (baste) a guideline round a corner of the linen 2.5 cm (1 in) in from the edge. The design begins 90 threads from the corner of the guideline. Work the cross stitch and backstitch over two threads using two strands of cotton.

1 To make up: trim the square to leave a 1.5 cm (⁵⁄8 in) seam allowance outside the cross stitch. Mitre the corners and turn a narrow hem. Slip stitch the corners and along the hem.

2 Work the same design in the corner diagonally opposite and press on the reverse side when complete.

3 Wrap blue thread round the card (cardboard) and make four tassels. Stitch these securely to each corner of the mat.

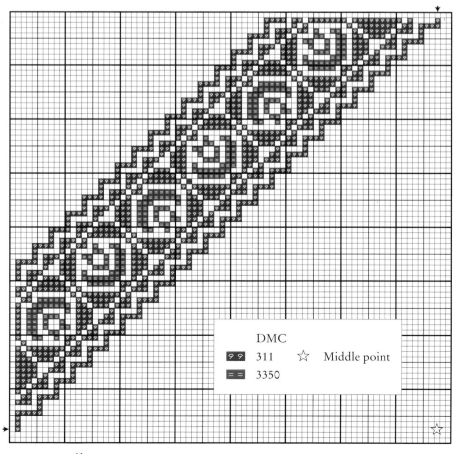

	DMC		
9 9	311	☆	Middle point
= =	3350		

CHINESE BOX

The tiger design on this box is adapted from a cylindrical Chinese seal from Hong Kong.

YOU WILL NEED

30 x 50 cm (12 x 20 in) white 25 count Lugana, Zweigart E3835

scissors

tacking (basting) thread

needle

stranded cotton Anchor 132, 403

tapestry needle

sewing thread

20 x 40 cm (8 x 16 in) thin card (cardboard)

adhesive tape

30 cm (12 in) square of blue lining fabric

all-purpose glue

WORKING THE CROSS STITCH

Cut a 13 x 25 cm (5 x 10 in) rectangle of evenweave and tack (baste) guidelines across the middle in both directions. Using two strands of cotton over two threads, outline the tigers in Holbein stitch (two rows of running stitch making a solid line). Fill in the cross stitch and work the Holbein stitch borders. Press the embroidered panel on the reverse side. Fold in half and stitch the short sides together close to the cross stitch to form a tube.

1 To make up: from thin card (cardboard) cut one 9 x 38 cm (3½ x 15 in) and one 10 x 19 cm (4 x 7½ in) rectangle. Curl the long piece round till the two ends meet and secure with tape. Tuck the tube inside the embroidered tube. Stick the raw edges to the inside. Cut a 15 x 22 cm (6 x 8½ in) piece of lining on the bias. Stitch the two short sides together. Curl the second piece of card round until it fits inside the embroidered tube and tape.

2 Put the lining inside the tube and stretch the fabric to the outside. Glue a turning of 12 mm (½ in) at the bottom and the larger area at the top. Cut two circles out of card to fit the bottoms of the tubes. Cover the smaller one with lining fabric and the larger with evenweave. Oversew the lining circle with the raw edges facing out and the evenweave with them facing in.

3 Cut a 2 x 38 cm (¾ x 15 in) strip of card. Curl it to fit loosely round the lip of the box. Make a fabric tube from a 6 x 22 cm (2⅜ x 8½ in) piece of evenweave. Fold it in half and tuck the tube inside. Stitch round the edge of the card through both layers. Cover a disc with linen as before and stitch round the ring, tucking the raw edges inside. Cut a disc to fit inside the lid and cover with lining fabric. Stick the disk on the inside to complete.

Anchor	Backstitch
▦ 132	— 403
	☆ Middle point

INDIAN NECK PURSE

This little bag is typical of those made by the nomadic Banjara people. The design layout was inspired by the wooden architecture in Gujarat.

YOU WILL NEED

two 15 x 18 cm (6 x 7 in) pieces of red 20 count evenweave linen

tacking (basting) thread

needle

interlocking bar frame

coton à broder no.16 DMC 321, 444, 552, 700, 796, 907, 943, 947

flower thread DMC 2333, 2531, 2797, 2907, 2917, 2947, 2956

tapestry needle

scissors

50 cm (20 in) of 90 cm (36 in) wide fine navy cotton

sewing machine

sewing thread

easy-turn rouleau maker or bodkin

pins

red wool

8 cm (3 in) square of card (cardboard)

WORKING THE CROSS STITCH

Experiment by mixing the different colours before working this exciting embroidery project. Subtle changes will occur depending on whether the dark or light thread is on top.

Tack (baste) vertical guidelines corresponding to the panels of the chart on both pieces of linen. The centre panel is worked in coton à broder and the borders in flower threads with each stitch worked over four threads.

Cut several 5 cm (2 in) wide bias strips of the navy cotton and stitch 8 mm (3/8 in) from the fold, then turn through to make rouleaux. Place the rouleaux in the spaces between the stitching and couch down with groups of two red cross stitches. Leave a border of eight threads round the cross stitch and trim the linen.

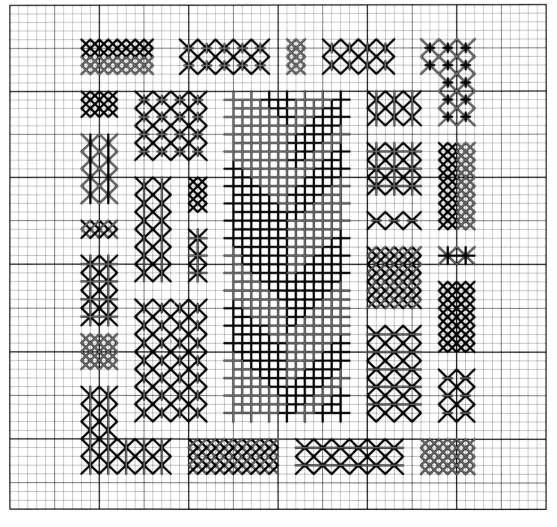

DMC	
—	light areas
—	dark areas

1 To make up: pin and tack each piece onto a 20 x 23 cm (8 x 9 in) rectangle of navy cotton. Machine stitch close to the edge. Mitre the corners of the backing fabric and turn a narrow hem onto the right side of the embroidery. Slip stitch in place.

2 With right sides facing out, oversew the two panels together down the sides and along the bottom.

3 Make three 1 m (39 in) lengths of rouleaux. Thread several strands of red wool through the centre of each to pad. Plait the rouleaux and knot the ends separately. Stitch the rouleaux together 8 cm (3 in) from the end by winding the cottons around the card (cardboard) and making a tassel over each knot. Sew the straps to the bag with cross stitches on the front and the back.

AFRICAN MASK

This stunning mask has been mounted in a long frame to give it the appearance of an African shield.

YOU WILL NEED

30 x 43 cm (12 x 17 in) khaki 28 count Annabelle, Zweigart E3240

tacking (basting) thread

needle

embroidery hoop (frame)

stranded cotton DMC 300, 301, 666, 712, 744, 783, 3371

light gold thread DMC Art.282

tapestry needle

24 x 36 cm (9½ x 14 in) mount board (backing board)

strong thread

picture frame

WORKING THE CROSS STITCH

Tack (baste) guidelines across the middle of the evenweave in both directions. Work the cross stitch design over two threads using two strands of cotton.

Although it will mean that you use all of the gold thread, you will get a more attractive finished piece if you separate the three strands and then put them together again before stitching. Finally, work the backstitch using a single strand of 3371.

1 To make up: press the embroidery on the wrong side. Stretch the fabric over the mount board (backing board) making sure it is centred, and fit into a picture frame of your choice.

DMC			
==	Art.282	//	783
:::	666	\\	712
>>	3371		
◇◇	300		**Backstitch**
↖↖	301	—	3371
▽▽	744	☆	Middle point

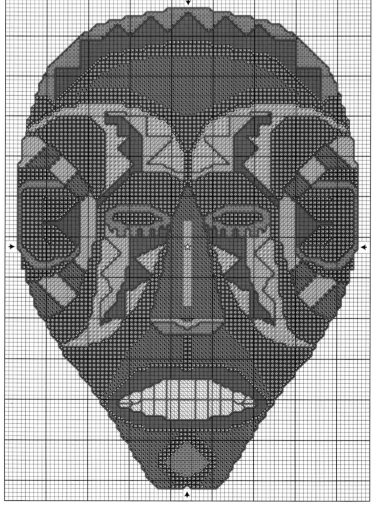

AFRICAN CUSHION

You could make a mini-cushion with this design, but with its fringe border it looks fantastic on a much larger cushion.

YOU WILL NEED

25 cm (10 in) square of 7 count Sudan canvas

rotating frame

tapestry wool Anchor 2 skeins each of 8006, 9490, 9564, 9648, 9800 and one of 9794

tapestry needle

42 x 94 cm (16½ x 37 in) cream furnishing fabric

scissors

pins

1.10 m (1¼ yd) natural fringing

sewing thread

sewing machine

40 cm (16 in) cushion pad

Anchor tapestry wool		
▬▬ 9800	◇◇ 9794	
⋮⋮ 9648	◤◥ 8006	
➤➤ 9564	▽▽ 9490	
☆ Middle point		

WORKING THE CROSS STITCH

Find the centre of the canvas and work the cross stitch as shown. Once complete, block the design to even out the stitches and trim the seam allowance to 1 cm (³⁄₈ in).

1 To make up: cut a 42 cm (16½ in) square of the cream fabric. Pin and tack (baste) the embroidery in the centre. Pin the fringing round the edge of the cross stitch. Trim and butt the ends of the fringe together taking care that they do not unravel. Tack carefully and stitch. Cut the other piece of cream fabric in half crossways and stitch a narrow hem down one short side of each piece.

2 Overlap the two hems and pin together to make a 42 cm (16½ in) square. Place the two cushion panels together with right sides facing and stitch. Trim the corners and turn through. Unravel the rest of the fringe and make four tassels with the short pieces of yarn. Sew one on each corner of the cushion and insert the cushion pad.

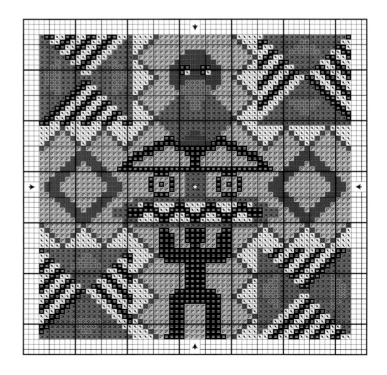

SKETCH BOOK COVER

Cover a sketch book for an artist friend.
The ribbon fastenings help to keep any cuttings or loose sketches safe.

YOU WILL NEED

30 x 40 cm (12 x 16 in) black 27 count Linda, Zweigart E1235

15 x 20 cm (6 x 8 in) sketch book

pins

tacking (basting) thread

needle

embroidery hoop (frame)

stranded cotton DMC 310, 321, 444

tapestry needle

scissors

double-sided tape

40 cm (16 in) fine red cord

sewing thread

WORKING THE CROSS STITCH

Fold the linen in half crossways and tuck the sketch book inside. Put a pin in to mark the centre of each side of the sketchbook and tack (baste) guidelines to mark the mid-point of the front cover. Work the cross stitch using three strands of cotton over two threads of linen. Once complete, work the backstitch using a single strand of black. Press on the reverse side.

DMC			
▄▄	310		Backstitch
▒▒	321	—	310
⟩⟩	444	☆	Middle point

1 To make up: lay the sketch book on the linen. Check that the embroidery is central and in line with the front cover and mark the corners with pins.

2 Cut across the corners 1 cm (3/8 in) from the sketch book. Put double-sided tape all round the inside cover. Hold the rest of the book upright and stick the linen onto the back of the cover, mitring each corner neatly and trimming away excess fabric if necessary.

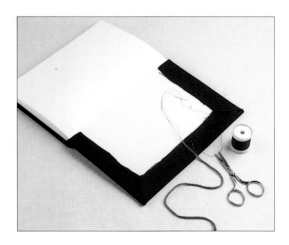

3 Finish the other side in the same way, making sure that the book closes easily. Cut the cord in two. Securely sew one piece in the middle of each inside cover. Slip stitch the mitred corners and stick the fly leaves down with double-sided tape to cover all the raw edges.

BUCKET BAG

The shape of this bag is based on a shigra basket from Ecuador.
The people there use it to carry fruit and vegetables.

YOU WILL NEED

60 x 84 cm (24 x 33 in) sand canvas fabric

scissors

tailor's chalk

Anchor Nordin 326, 341, 365

embroidery needle

pins

tacking (basting) thread

needle

sewing thread

sewing machine

1 m 60 cm (1¾ yd) thick cord

Anchor Nordin	
——	326
——	341
——	365

WORKING THE CROSS STITCH

This project is unusual because the cross stitch is worked on ordinary canvas. The weave on canvas is quite prominent and it is quite easy to follow the grain. With a little practice you will be able to make evenly sized and spaced stitches.

Cut two 30 x 63 cm (12 x 25 in) rectangles. Fold one piece in half

lengthways and mark the fold line with chalk. Work a row of spaced cross stitches in 326, 2 cm (¾ in) either side of the chalk line. Work the single cross stitches and fish motifs between the lines. Work parallel rows of cross stitch 8 cm (3 in) from the raw edge, then finish the other six stitches of the vertical lines to complete the design.

1 To make up: with right sides together stitch the short seams of both panels to form a tube. Cut two 20 cm (8 in) circles from the canvas. Pin one circle to the bottom of each tube, easing the fabric as you go. Tack (baste) and stitch round the base. Snip into the curves and turn the embroidered piece through to the right side.

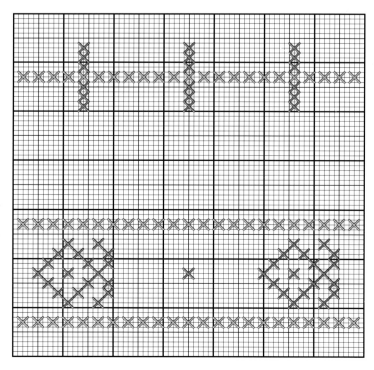

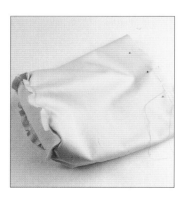

2 Cut the cord in two and pin one piece 6 cm (2½ in) to either side of the centre back seam, with the loop facing towards the bag. Pin the other strap on the opposite side and stitch securely inside the seam allowance.

3 Tuck the lining inside the bag and fold over the top edge of both pieces by about 1.5 cm (⅝ in). Pin and tack the layers together and stitch close to the top edge. Stitch again 5 mm (¼ in) away to finish.

MEXICAN TOY BAG

FOLK ART

Toddlers will be delighted to help tidy their bricks into this big strong bag.

YOU WILL NEED

18 x 46 cm (7 x 18 in) antique white 20 count Bellana, Zweigart E3256

tacking (basting) thread

needle

stranded cotton DMC 300, 310, 349, 603, 704, 806, 972

tapestry needle

80 x 60 cm (32 x 24 in) navy heavyweight twill fabric

scissors

pins

sewing machine

sewing thread

1.60 m (1¾ yd) thick white cord

safety pin

comb

DMC		
== 972	◥◥	310
⋮⋮⋮ 704	▽▽	603
⋗⋗ 300	◢◢	806
◇◇ 349	Backstitch	
	— 310	

WORKING THE CROSS STITCH

Tack (baste) guidelines across the middle of the evenweave. Work the cross stitch design using two strands of cotton over single threads, then work the backstitch. Press gently on the reverse side when complete.

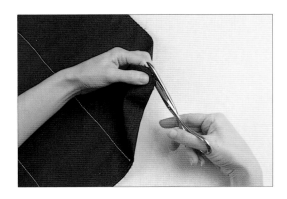
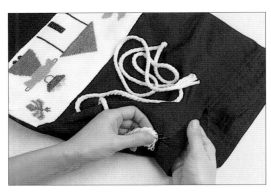

1 To make up: cut the navy fabric in two, crossways. Turn in the long edges of the embroidered panel and pin it 15 cm (6 in) from the bottom of one piece of fabric. Tack (baste) and stitch the two long sides. With right sides facing, pin the pieces together down the sides and bottom. Stitch, leaving a 4 cm (1½ in) gap on both sides 7 cm (2¾ in) from the top. Zig-zag close to the stitching, then trim and turn through.

2 Fold over the top edge and make a 5 cm (2 in) hem. Pin and sew the hem in place and then top stitch 1 cm (½ in) down from the top fold line. Cut the cord in half. Using a large safety pin, thread the pieces of cord through the casing in opposite directions. Tie the ends together 8 cm (3 in) from the end to form a tassel. Unravel the threads, comb them out and trim neatly to finish.

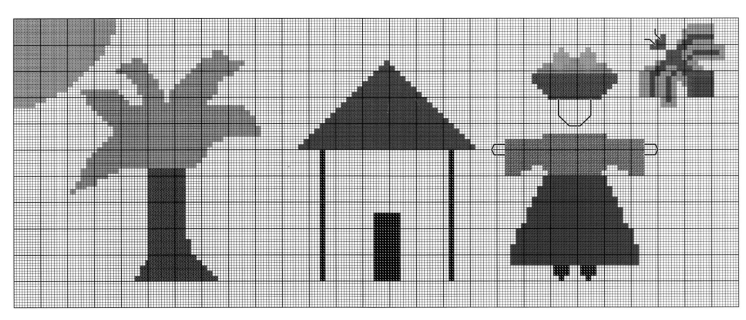

SHOE BAG

Geometric weaving designs can be adapted quite easily into cross stitch. These stylized animals come from a hammock made in Ghana.

YOU WILL NEED

28 x 66 cm (11 x 26 in) golden tan 28 count Quaker evenweave linen

scissors

tacking (basting) thread

needle

stranded cotton DMC 300, 498, 676, 919, 976

tapestry needle

pins

sewing machine

sewing thread

safety pin

WORKING THE CROSS STITCH

Cut a 5 x 66 cm (2 x 26 in) strip from the fabric for the cord. Fold the larger piece in half both ways and tack (baste) along the folds. Work the cross stitch using two strands of cotton over two threads. Begin at the bottom of the chart, working the cockerel above the crossways tacking. Press on the wrong side when complete.

1 To make up: fold the fabric in half with the embroidery facing in. Pin and stitch the two side seams, leaving a 5 cm (2 in) gap on one side 2.5 cm (1 in) from the top. Press the seams open.

2 To make the casing, fold over 5 cm (2 in) at the top. Turn under 12 mm (1/2 in), then pin and stitch in place. Stitch again close to the top edge.

3 Press the long edges of the reversed fabric strip into the centre. Turn the ends in 12 mm (1/2 in) and then fold the strip lengthways again. Pin and stitch round all sides. Thread the strap through the casing with a safety pin and stitch the ends together securely. Pull the joined ends through to the other side of the bag to complete the project.

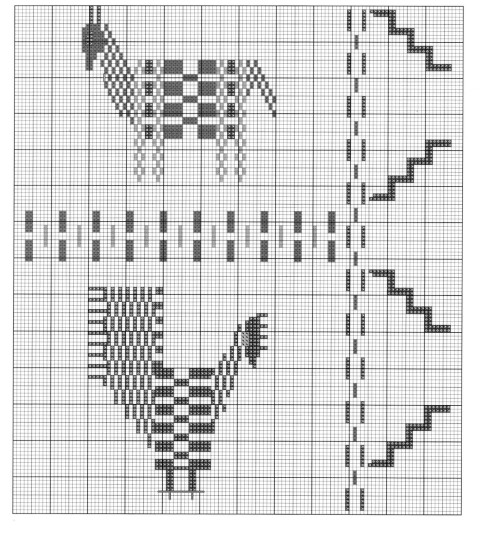

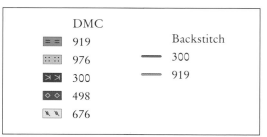

	DMC		Backstitch
═ ═	919	──	300
⋮ ⋮	976	──	919
▷ ▷	300		
◇ ◇	498		
✖ ✖	676		

MEXICAN WALLHANGING

This little hanging was inspired by traditional Mexican God's eyes.
Why not make one or two more to hang alongside it?

WORKING THE CROSS STITCH

Cut two 18 x 25 cm (7 x 10 in)
rectangles of linen. Tack (baste) a
guideline lengthways down the middle
of one piece. Tack a second line across
the linen, 10 cm (4 in) from the top.
Work the cross stitch and backstitch
using two strands of cotton over two
threads of linen. Press on the reverse
side when complete.

1 To make up: cut two 5 x 13 cm (2 x 5
in) rectangles of linen. Fold each in
half lengthways and stitch a 12 mm (½ in)
seam allowance. Press the seams open
and turn through. Position the seams at
the centre back and press again.

2 Fold the tabs in half with the seam
to the inside and pin along the top
edge, on either side of the embroidered
panel. Pin the two pieces of linen
together, with the embroidery and tabs
to the inside, and stitch along the top and
down both sides. Trim the seams and
corners and turn through.

3 Fray the bottom edge of the hanging
and press on the reverse side. Slip
the twig through the tabs and tie the cord
at each end to hang.

YOU WILL NEED

36 cm (14 in) square of 32
count natural evenweave linen

scissors

tacking (basting) thread

needle

small embroidery frame
(flexihoop)

stranded cotton DMC 310, 435,
550, 701, 712, 743, 900

tapestry needle

sewing machine

sewing thread

pins

15 cm (6 in) twig

30 cm (12 in) fine cord

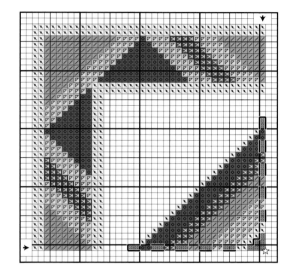

DMC		
⬚ 435	◢ 900	
▶ 550		
◆ 701	Backstitch	
✕ 712	— 310	
▽ 743	☆ Middle point	

INDIAN MOBILE

Shisha mirrors are traditionally hung to protect against evil, in the belief that any spirit seeing its reflection will be terrified and flee.

YOU WILL NEED

two sheets of dark green stitching paper, Jane Greenoff's Inglestone collection

stranded cotton DMC 3 skeins of 783 and 796, 4 skeins of 911 and 1 skein of 815 and 3765

tapestry needle

scissors

1.5 cm (⅝ in) square of thin card (cardboard)

30 cm (12 in) piano wire

WORKING THE CROSS STITCH

Stitching paper is prone to tear but it can be repaired with sticky tape and the holes repunched with a large needle. Work the different motifs and their mirror images onto the stitching paper using three strands of cotton, and leaving spaces for the shisha mirrors. Apply the mirrors as shown in the techniques section and then fill in any spaces with cross stitch.

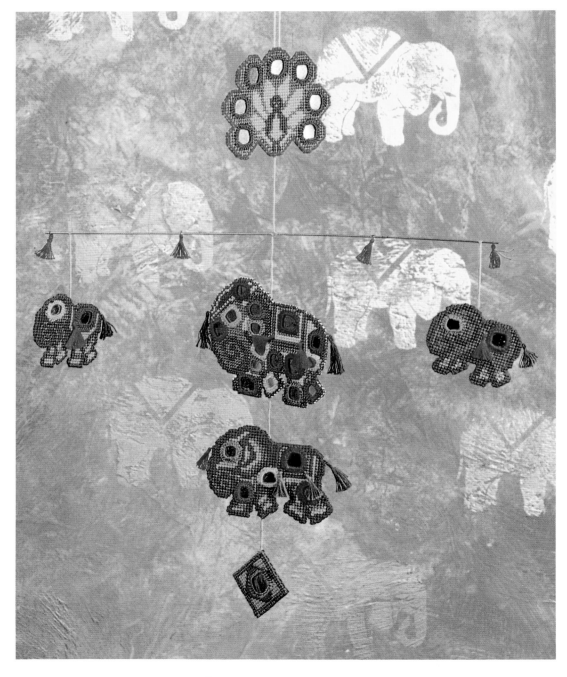

1 To make up: cut out the different motifs taking care not to snip the stitches. Oversew the two halves together using a single strand of cotton. Separate strands of cotton and make some 1.5 cm (⅝ in) mini-tassels for the elephants. Sew three on each side of the larger elephants and two on the smaller ones. Sew a tassel on one corner of the diamond motif.

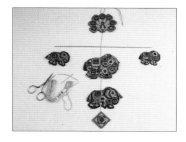

2 Lay out the pieces of the mobile on a flat surface, leaving gaps of about 4 cm (1½ in). Use all six strands of yellow cotton to hold the mobile together. Loop a 20 cm (8 in) length onto the wire. Sew one end to the bottom of the peacock and the other end to the back of the largest elephant. Stitch the other large elephant and the diamond underneath. Loop three strands of cotton over the ends of the wire and stitch the little elephants in place. Complete the mobile with some tassels and stitch a loop for hanging to the back of the peacock.

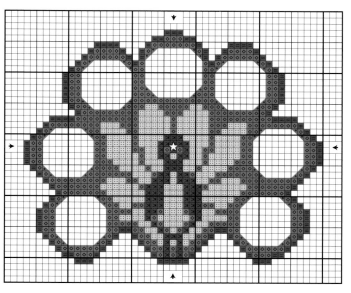

Peacock motif

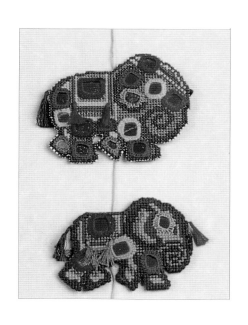

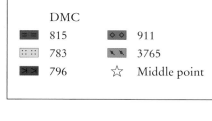

DMC

== ==	815	◇ ◇	911
∴∴ ∴∴	783	⊠ ⊠	3765
► ►	796	☆	Middle point

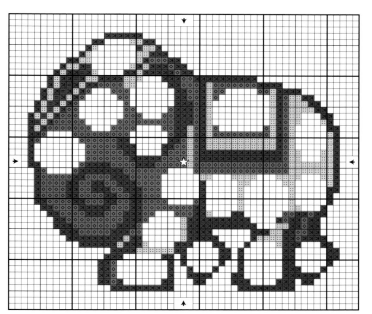

Large elephant motif

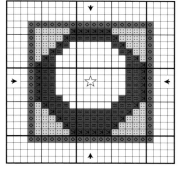

Diamond motif

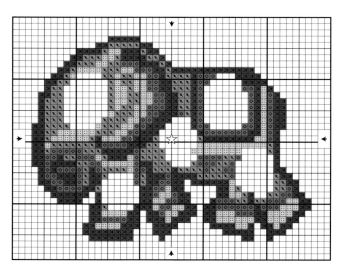

Left: medium elephant   Above: small elephant

NAPKIN RING AND TABLE MAT

This elaborate design was adapted from the yoke of a dress stitched and worn by the nomadic Baluchi people of western Pakistan.

YOU WILL NEED

8 x 22 cm (3 x 8½ in) black 18 count Aida for each napkin ring

25 x 36 cm (10 x 14 in) black 18 count Aida for each table mat

tacking (basting) thread

needle

embroidery hoop (frame)

stranded cotton DMC 349, 352, 3731, 3733

tapestry needle

sewing thread

scissors

NAPKIN RING

WORKING THE CROSS STITCH

Tack (baste) a guideline down the centre of the Aida. Using two strands of cotton, stitch three full diamonds with a half diamond at each end.

1 To make up: turn under the top and bottom edges by 5 mm (¼ in) and oversew invisibly on the wrong side. Trim the ends of the band to 5 mm (¼ in) turn under and slip stitch together from the right side.

TABLE MAT

WORKING THE CROSS STITCH

Tack (baste) a guideline round the bottom right hand corner of the Aida 5 cm (2 in) in from the edge. Work three complete diamonds using two strands of cotton.

1 To make up: mitre the corners and turn a small 5 mm (¼ in) hem to the reverse side. Tack in position then machine or hand stitch to finish.

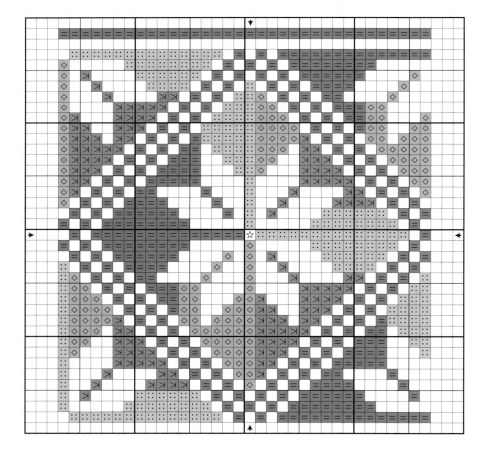

DMC		
= = 349	◇◇	3733
∷∷ 352		
➤➤ 3731	☆	Middle point

INDIAN PICTURE FRAME

Indian embroidery is worked in rich colours and often incorporates different animal motifs. One of the most traditional is the elephant.

YOU WILL NEED

sheet of 7 count plastic canvas

stranded cotton Anchor three skeins of 70 and one each of 150, 254, 258, 304, 307, 1006

tapestry needle

needle

scissors

25 x 30 cm (10 x 12 in) mount board (backing board)

pencil

13 cm (5 in) picture

spray mount

all-purpose glue

small brass ring

sewing thread

WORKING THE CROSS STITCH

The cross stitches in this design are worked with the top stitch direction changing in alternate rows to give the embroidery more texture. Work the cross stitch using all six strands of cotton. You will achieve better coverage of the canvas if the threads are separated and then recombined before stitching.

1 To make up: once the cross stitch is complete, cut out the centre panel and trim the sides. Oversew the edges in two directions to form cross stitches which will cover the edges of the plastic canvas.

2 Mark the size of the frame opening on the mount board (backing board). Spray mount a picture of your choice in position and glue the frame on top. Sew a small brass ring near the top of the frame to hang it by.

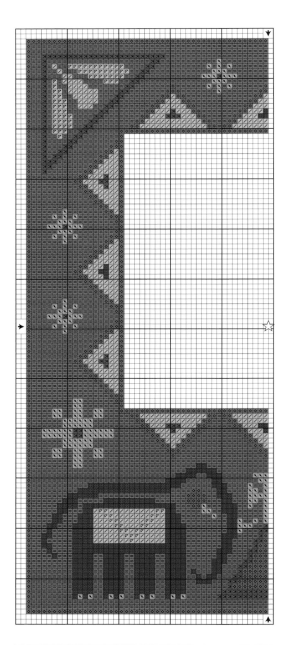

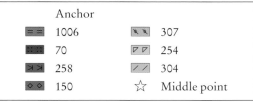

Anchor			
＝＝	1006		307
	70	▽▽	254
▶▶	258	∕∕	304
◆◆	150	☆	Middle point

INDIAN MIRROR FRAME

This little mirror frame has been given a rich textured finish with the addition of shisha mirrors and silver beads.

YOU WILL NEED

20 cm (8 in) square of 10 count single thread canvas

stranded cotton Anchor 316, 403, 9046

tapestry needle

four shisha mirrors

double-sided tape

sixteen 5 mm (¼ in) silver beads

11 cm (4¼ in) square of mount board (backing board)

12.5 cm (5 in) square of mount board

30 x 56 cm (12 x 22 in) black cotton fabric

10 cm (4 in) mirror

scissors

pins

sewing thread

needle

5 cm (2 in) black tape

WORKING THE CROSS STITCH

Work the red cross stitch using a double thickness of stranded cotton. Complete the black stitching, leaving space in each corner for the shisha.

1 To make up: stick the shisha onto the canvas with double-sided tape and attach using six strands of black. Sew the beads on with two strands of cotton. Work the orange cross stitch using double thickness stranded cotton.

2 Cover both pieces of mount board (backing board) with black fabric and stick the mirror in the middle of the larger square. Cut out the centre panel of the canvas, leaving 12 mm (½ in) and snip into the corners. Turn under the edges of the embroidered canvas and pin onto the large square of covered mount board. Oversew round all sides.

3 To make the stand, cut a piece of black fabric 2 cm (¾ in) larger than the small covered square. Turn under 1 cm (⅜ in) all round and oversew to the reverse side. Oversew the stand to the mirror frame along one edge and stitch a small piece of tape between the two, at the other end, for support.

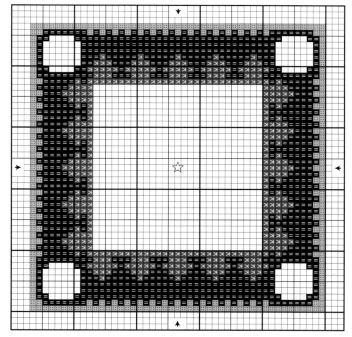

Anchor	■ ■ 403	▶ ▶ 9046
	⋯ 316	☆ Middle point

INDIAN HANGINGS

Indian embroidery often incorporates shisha mirrors to ward off evil spirits but large sequins can be equally effective.

YOU WILL NEED

one sheet of stitching paper, Jane Greenoff's Inglestone collection

stranded cotton DMC 436, 469, 738, 744, 783, 796, 806, 824, 915, 917, 918, 920, 922

tapestry needle

1.5 cm (⅝ in) shisha or sequins

2.5 cm (1 in) shisha or sequins

double-sided tape

scissors

pins

sewing thread

needle

small bells

1.5 cm (⅝ in) square of card (cardboard)

WORKING THE CROSS STITCH

Stitch the motifs using three strands of cotton, leaving spaces as indicated for the shisha.

These designs are intended to hang against the wall. If they are to hang free both sides will have to be stitched.

Stitching paper is apt to tear if stitches are unpicked but it can be repaired with sticky tape and the holes repunched with a large needle.

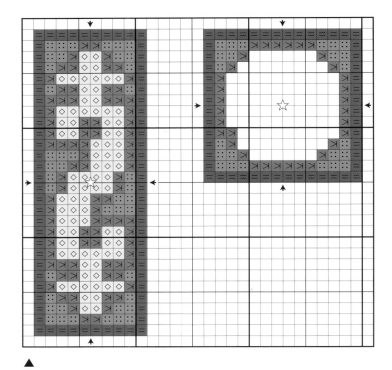

DMC			
▬▬ 824	▸▸ 806	☆ Middle point	
⠿ 469	◇◇ 744		

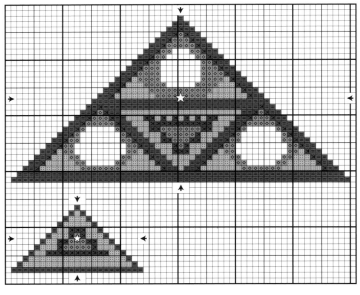

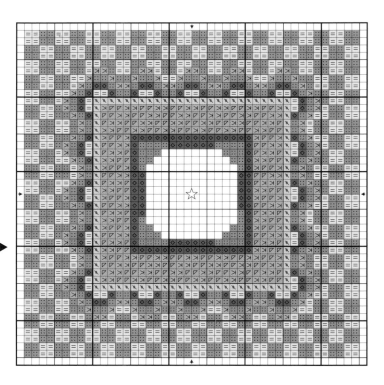

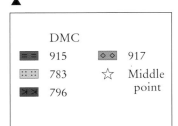

DMC	
▬▬ 915	◇◇ 917
⠿ 783	☆ Middle point
▸▸ 796	

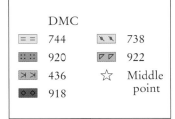

DMC	
══ 744	◣◣ 738
⠿ 920	▽▽ 922
▸▸ 436	☆ Middle point
◆◆ 918	

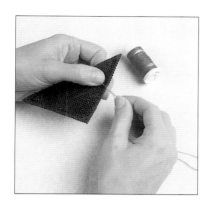

1 To make up: stick the shisha into the spaces and attach as shown in the techniques section. Fill in any spaces round the edge with cross stitch. Cut out the motifs close to the stitching, taking care not to cut any of the threads. Cut a piece of stitching paper to the correct size for each decoration and pin onto the reverse side. Oversew the edges using a single strand of cotton.

2 Assemble the decoration by oversewing the shapes together and winding a thread between the shapes several times to make a "neck" before finishing off. Sew tiny bells on in the same way. Complete the decoration with some tiny tassels, made using single strands of cotton wrapped round the card (cardboard).

TEMPLATES

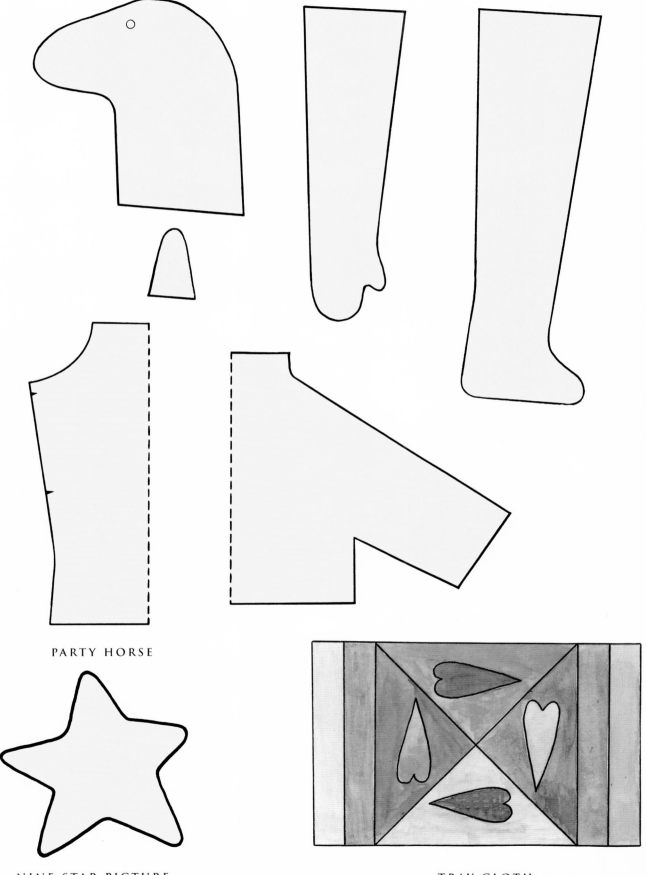

PARTY HORSE

NINE STAR PICTURE

TRAY CLOTH